EASY JAZZIN' ABOUT
very easy fun pieces for
PIANO/KEYBOARD

CONTENTS

© 1993 by Faber Music Ltd
First published in 1993 by Faber Music Ltd
3 Queen Square London WC1N 3AU
Cover by velladesign
Music engraved by John Walsh
Printed in England by Caligraving Ltd
All rights reserved
ISBN 0-571-51337-9

PAM WEDGWOOD

ff FABER MUSIC

£7.50

1. Steady as a Rock

KEY: G major
STYLE: Rock 'n' roll

Workouts for the Right Hand

This pattern occurs throughout the piece:

Clap then play: 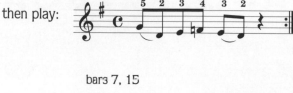 detach the two middle notes.

bars 7, 15

Clap then play:

bar 23

Clap then play:

Workouts for the Left Hand

This pattern occurs throughout the piece:

Clap then play:

bars 7, 15

Clap then play:

bar 23

Clap then play:

Useful Hints

Play this piece with a **very strong** beat.

Make sure you observe all **accent** marks > > >.

Bars 17-20 should be played very **legato** (smoothly).

Don't forget to play **all expression marks**.

Rhythmic accompaniment

Use a rock 'n' roll drum beat.

1. Steady as a Rock

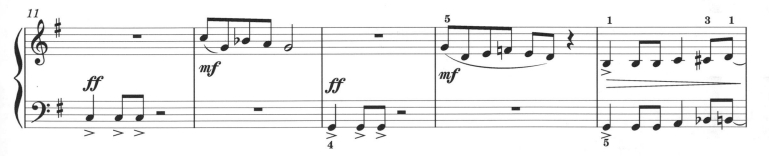

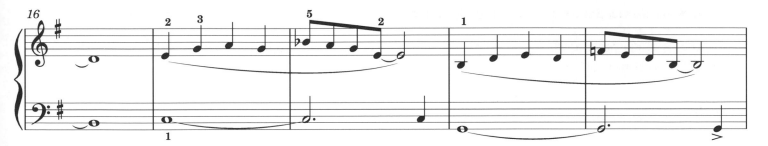

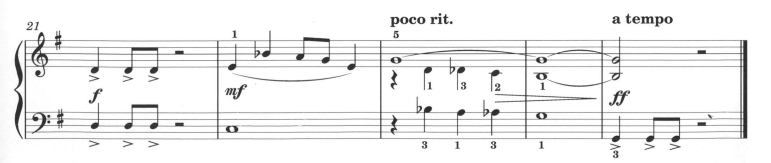

2. Test Drive

KEY: D minor
STYLE: Disco

Workouts for the Right Hand

Clap then play:

Try to clap this difficult little rhythm:

bars 9, 10

Now play it (pay special attention to your fingering!):

etc.

Try to clap this pattern – it occurs many times:
How many times does this pattern occur?

Workouts for the Left Hand

Always play the left hand with a good accent where indicated:

etc.

Useful Hints

Accurate fingerwork at all times!

D.S. means **Dal Segno**, i.e. go back to the sign 𝄋.

D.S. 𝄋 al ⊕ poi al Coda means go back to the sign 𝄋 until you reach the Coda sign ⊕ – then play the CODA section (the bit on the end!)

Rhythmic Accompaniment

Use a disco drum beat.

2. Test Drive

With a lively disco beat ♩=132 (30 m.p.h)

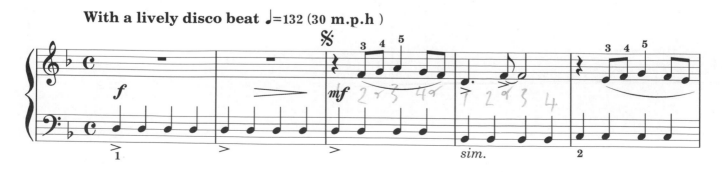

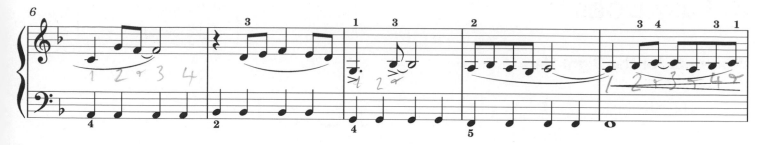

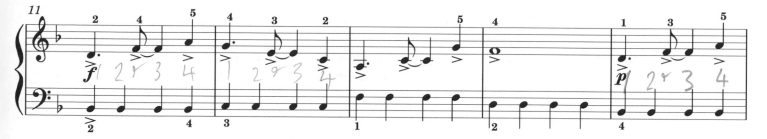

D.S. 𝄋 *al* ⊕ *poi al Coda* **CODA**

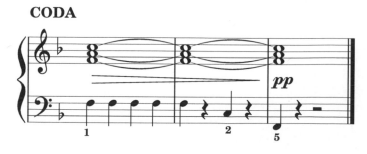

3. Easy Does It

| KEY: C major |
| STYLE: Swing |

Workouts for the Right Hand

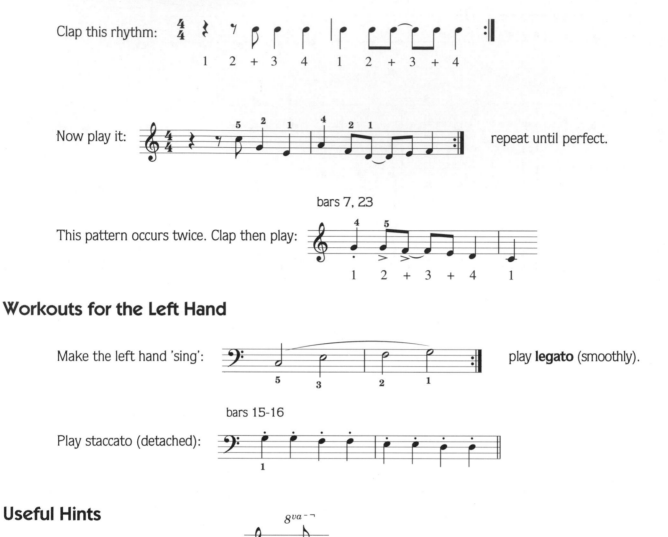

Clap this rhythm:

repeat until perfect.

bars 7, 23

This pattern occurs twice. Clap then play:

Workouts for the Left Hand

Make the left hand 'sing':

play **legato** (smoothly).

bars 15-16

Play staccato (detached):

Useful Hints

On the last bar you will notice   = play one octave higher than written.

Play this as the title suggests, with ease - don't rush - let the music swing along.

Rhythmic accompaniment

Swing

3. Easy Does It

4. 5th Avenue

KEY: F major

STYLE: Slow, with a lot of expression

Workouts for the Right Hand

You will notice that the first three bars of this piece are based on the interval of a 5th: 5 notes between the bottom and the top. How many 5ths can you find in **5th Avenue**?

Try this exercise in 5ths:

bars 15, 16

Repeat until perfect!

Workouts for the Left Hand

Playing 5ths in the left hand:

Useful Hints

The **Pedal** (right, or sustaining pedal) features in this piece. Try this exercise (lift when you see ⌃ then down again):

Make your performance of **5th Avenue** sound full of your own expression.

Poco rit = a little slower.

A tempo = back to the original speed.

Rhythmic accompaniment

Use a slow 8 or 16 drum beat.

4. 5th Avenue

5. Strawberry Flip

KEY: C major

STYLE: Reggae (a strongly rhythmic type of West Indian music)

Workouts for the Right Hand

Practice bars 10-11:

Workouts for the Left Hand

Useful Hints

Keep your **left hand** in position.

Make sure you are playing the dotted quavers correctly.

Clap:

Observe all **accent** marks >.

Rhythmic accompaniment

Reggae drum beat.

5. Strawberry Flip

In a lively, reggae style ♩=116

6. Motorway Blues

KEY: F major
STYLE: Slow blues

Workouts for the Right Hand

Clap then play:

Fingering change:

Triplet exercise: repeat until perfect!

Dotted work-out. Clap:

Workouts for the Left Hand

Play this very smoothly and quietly. Make it 'sing':

Drive the bass along (intervals of a 5th to a 6th):

Useful Hints

Play in a very relaxed tempo.

Make up your own words to fit.

Observe all **expression marks**.

Crescendo (cresc.) = gradually getting **louder**.

Rhythmic Accompaniment

Blues or slow swing.

6. Motorway Blues

7. Funk It!

KEY: A minor
STYLE: Funky

Workouts for the Right Hand

Clap this rhythm pattern (note the time changes). Then try to play it.

Workouts for the Left Hand

Try counting in a slow 8:

Repeat until perfect.

Useful Hints

1st and 2nd time bars:

first time through play 1st time bar and repeat, second time go on to the 2nd time bar.

D.S. 𝄇 al ⊕ poi al Coda = go back to the sign 𝄇, until you reach this sign ⊕, then go straight to the Coda.

Rhythmic accompaniment

Funky drum beat.

7. Funk It!

In a funky style ♩=108

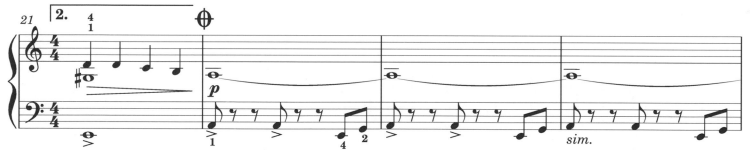

8. Songbird

| KEY: G major |
| STYLE: Light rock |

Workouts for the Right Hand

Finger strengtheners for bar 3:

bar 16

Clap then play:

1 2 3 4   1 + 2 + 3 + 4   1 2 + 3 + 4 +

Workouts for the Left Hand

bar 9

Hold for 4 counts

bars 16-20

Useful Hints

Keep the right hand very **legato** – try to imagine 'singing' it.

Make your own song using bars 1-8 as the intro. Your song begins at bar 9.

Make up your own words for **Songbird**.

Rhythmic Accompaniment

Moderate 8-beat drum setting.

8. Songbird

9. Harry's Theme

KEY: D major

STYLE: Rock

Workouts for the Right Hand

Think about your fingering:

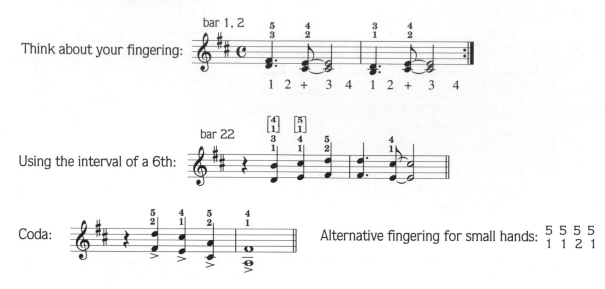

Using the interval of a 6th:

Coda:

Alternative fingering for small hands: 5 5 5 5 / 1 1 2 1

Workouts for the Left Hand

Fingering pattern:

bars 22-28

Useful Hints

Play with very strong accents: pay special attention to the opening rhythmic line.

Poco rit. = a little slower.

D.C. (**Da Capo**) = go back to the beginning.

Rhythmic Accompaniment

Lively Rock drum-beat.

9. Harry's Theme

10. Forget-Me-Not

KEY: C major
STYLE: Descriptive, with a good legato feel throughout

Workouts for the Right Hand

In the middle section you will find some notes written on **Leger Lines**. Let's identify them:

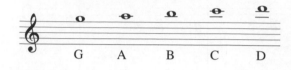

G   A   B   C   D

Now try them in the written passage:

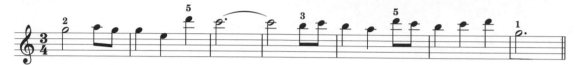

Workout for the Left Hand

Bars 9-11 are written in the treble clef, before returning to the bass clef in bar 12:

Useful Hints

Try to join all your notes smoothly – **legato**.

Work at this piece in sections, until each is perfect: bars 1-8, 9-16, 17-23, 24-28.

Rhythmic Accompaniment

Fairly gentle waltz drum beat.

10. Forget-Me-Not

11. Champagne Rag

KEY: F major
STYLE: Ragtime

Workouts for the Right Hand

Bar 1:

Bar 2:

Bars 3-4:

Bars 5-8:

Workouts for the Left Hand

Bars 1-4:

Useful Hints

Never play ragtime fast! Just bouncy!

Try this rhythm work-out:

bar 9

Tap with LH

Rhythmic Accompaniment

Ragtime drum beat (steady).

11. Champagne Rag

The JAZZIN' ABOUT Series

PAM WEDGWOOD

Christmas Jazzin' About. Piano   ISBN 0-571-51507-X

Christmas Jazzin' About. Piano Duet   ISBN 0-571-51584-3

Christmas Jazzin' About. Violin   ISBN 0-571-51694-7

Christmas Jazzin' About. Cello   ISBN 0-571-51695-5

Christmas Jazzin' About. Flute   ISBN 0-571-51586-X

Christmas Jazzin' About. Clarinet   ISBN 0-571-51585-1

Christmas Jazzin' About. Alto Saxophone   ISBN 0-571-51587-8

Christmas Jazzin' About. Trumpet   ISBN 0-571-51696-3

Easy Jazzin' About. Piano   ISBN 0-571-51337-9

Easy Jazzin' About. Piano Duets   ISBN 0-571-51661-0

Green Jazzin' About. Piano   ISBN 0-571-51645-9

Jazzin' About. Piano   ISBN 0-571-51105-8

Jazzin' About. Piano Duets   ISBN 0-571-51662-9

Jazzin' About. Violin   ISBN 0-571-51315-8

Jazzin' About. Cello   ISBN 0-571-51316-6

Jazzin' About. Flute   ISBN 0-571-51275-5

Jazzin' About. Clarinet   ISBN 0-571-51273-9

Jazzin' About. Alto Saxophone   ISBN 0-571-51054-X

Jazzin' About. Trumpet   ISBN 0-571-51039-6

Jazzin' About. Trombone   ISBN 0-571-51053-1

Jazzin' About Styles. Piano   ISBN 0-571-51718-8

More Jazzin' About. Piano   ISBN 0-571-51437-5

Really Easy Jazzin' About. Piano   ISBN 0-571-52089-8

FABER *ff* MUSIC